Why Don't Polar Bears Have Stripes?

By Katherine Smith

Consultant: Nicola Davies

WATERBIRD BOOKS

Columbus, Ohio

![Mc Graw Hill] **Children's Publishing**

This edition published in the United States of America in 2004 by
Waterbird Books
an imprint of McGraw-Hill Children's Publishing,
a Division of The McGraw-Hill Companies
8787 Orion Place
Columbus, Ohio 43240-4027

www.MHkids.com

Library of Congress Cataloging-in-Publication Data is on file with the publisher.

First published in Great Britain in 2004 by *ticktock* Media Ltd.,
Unit 2, Orchard Business Centre, North Farm Road, Tunbridge Wells, Kent TN3 3XF.
Text and illustrations © 2004 *ticktock* Entertainment Ltd.
We would like to thank: Meme Ltd. and Elizabeth Wiggans.
Every effort has been made to trace the copyright holders, and we apologize in advance for any unintentional omissions.
We would be pleased to insert the appropriate acknowledgements in any subsequent edition of this publication.

Printed in China

1-57768-946-1

1 2 3 4 5 6 7 8 9 10 TTM 09 08 07 06 05 04

CONTENTS

Any words appearing in the text in bold, **like this**, are explained in the Glossary.

Why don't polar bears have stripes?

Because polar bears live in the icy **Arctic**, where everything is white.

Polar bears wash themselves with snow. They lick their coats to stay clean.

Polar bears stay hidden when they hunt for food. Their white fur allows them to blend into the white ice and snow. This is called **camouflage**.

This Arctic fox uses camouflage to blend into its background.

Polar bear **cubs** have whiter fur than adult bears.

The Arctic is the cold region around the North Pole. Much of the Arctic does not get sun during the winter months.

Why don't polar bears freeze in the cold Arctic air?

Because polar bears have thick layers of fat to keep them warm.

This thick layer of fat is called **blubber**. It protects the bears from the freezing cold, even when they swim in icy water! Their thick, white fur also keeps them warm.

Black skin under their white fur soaks up heat from the sun. This helps keep the bears warm.

Each hair in a polar bear's fur is hollow and traps heat. This also helps to keep the polar bear warm.

After swimming, bears shake themselves like dogs to dry off.

Why don't polar bears live in large groups?

13

Because there is a lot of competition for food in the Arctic.

Few plants and animals can survive in the Arctic, so there isn't much food. It is much easier for a polar bear to find a meal when other hungry bears are not around!

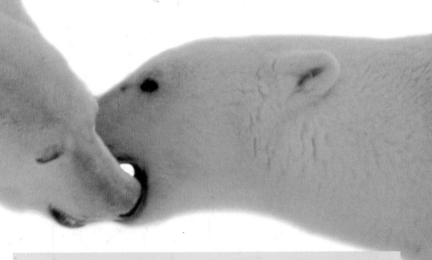

Polar bears gather together when there is a lot of food in one place.

If there is enough food, polar bears will share it with each other.

Male polar bears live on their own.

Female polar bears and their cubs keep away from male bears. This is because males sometimes attack their cubs.

Why aren't polar bears born underwater?

Because polar bears are mammals and, like almost all mammals, give birth to their young on land.

Whales, dolphins, and porpoises are the only mammals that give birth underwater. Polar bears give birth to their cubs in dens under the snow. They are safe there from the winter cold and from **predators**. The bears and their cubs sleep until they leave the den in the spring.

Polar bears usually have two cubs.

Cubs feed on their mother's milk until they are two years old. Then, they hunt for their own food.

At birth, a cub weighs only about one pound. That is the same as three or four apples!

Why don't polar bears climb trees?

Because there is only freezing ice and water in the Arctic.

No trees can grow in the frozen ice of the Arctic. Polar bear cubs spend their time sliding on the snow and ice and wrestling or "play-fighting!"

Play-fighting helps polar bear cubs learn to fight for real.

After a long play, polar bear cubs may curl up together for a nap.

Most people will not travel to the Arctic. So, polar bears have been brought into **captivity** so that people can see them and learn about them.

Why don't polar bears eat fruit and berries?

Because polar bears are **carnivores**, and they eat only meat.

Polar bears hunt mainly seals. Hidden by their camouflage, the polar bears sneak up on their **prey**. Then, they rush at their prey before it can escape into the sea.

Polar bears also eat fish, seabirds, and other small mammals.

Polar bears can swim up to 25 miles between **ice floes** in search of food.

Polar bears have big paws with sharp claws for grabbing prey.

A polar bear will wait by a seal's breathing hole in the ice. When the seal comes up to breathe, the bear will grab it!

Polar bear
PROFILE

Life span

25–30 years.

Size

6 ½–7 feet. That is one-and-a-half times as tall as a male human being!

Weight

Male bear: 1,500 pounds or more. That is about as heavy as eight male human beings!
Female bear: Up to 550 pounds – that's about as heavy as three male human beings!

Numbers

There are between 25,000 and 40,000 polar bears in the Arctic.

28

Polar bears
live in the Arctic.

Fact file

Scientists call the polar bear *Ursus maritimus*. It means *sea bear* in Latin.

Scientists think that polar bears can see well underwater. They can spot food 15 feet away.

Polar bears' front paws are partly webbed to help them swim.

Polar bears have been known to swim 60 miles without stopping.

In 1979, three polar bears at the San Diego Zoo turned green. Scientists discovered that a type of green water plant was living in their fur.

GLOSSARY

Arctic
The area around the North Pole.

Blubber
A thick layer of fat that protects an animal against the cold.

Camouflage
Colorings or markings on an animal or insect that allow it to blend in with its natural surroundings.

Captivity
When an animal is held in a place that is not its natural environment. Animals living in the zoo or in a preserve are in captivity.

Carnivores
Plants or animals that feed on the meat of other animals.

Cub

The name for a polar bear baby. It is also used for the young of bears, foxes and lions.

Ice floes

Sheets of floating ice.

Mammals

Animals that are warm-blooded and produce milk for their young.

Predator

An animal that survives by hunting, killing, and eating other animals.

Prey

An animal that is hunted for food by another animal.

INDEX

Voca 2